~~My~~ Skip's Dog, Lola

Skip's ~~My~~ Dog, Lola

by
Liz Ciufo

Copyright 2024
Liz Ciufo

 Dog, Lola

ISBN: 978-1-7355521-6-3
eISBN: 978-1-7355521-7-0

No part of this publication may be reproduced, distributed, or transmitted in any form or by any means, including photocopying, recording, or other electronic or mechanical methods without the prior written permission of the author, except in the case of brief quotations embodied in critical reviews and certain other noncommercial uses permitted by copyright law.

Printed in the United States

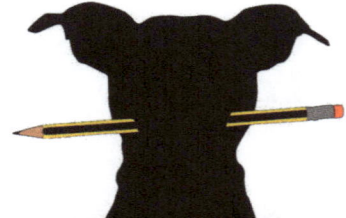

This book is dedicated to the memory of Marine Sergeant Mike Halley, for his service to his country in Vietnam and later for his service to his fellow veterans through the K9s for Veterans program.

FOREWORD
BY BEVERLY "DrBev" JACKSON

DrBev is a National Certified Counselor, Licensed Mental Health Counselor, and a Certified Gestalt Psychotherapist. She is the President and Educational Director of DrBev Mental Health Counseling, as well as an author, radio and TV personality, and seminar and workshop facilitator.

I met Jessica, a young, precocious, pre-teenager with a wonderful, gracious smile, at Halley's K9s for Veterans as a volunteer in 2011. Halley's K9s for Veterans occupied a huge compound surrounded by a fortress-like fence in an area of Tampa, Florida, that some would say may not be comfortable for a young girl not familiar with life on that side of town. As I watched the process of a new veteran or dog enter into the camp, Jessica appeared to me as if she were in her natural habitat with the dogs and the veterans, as well as the people who lived in the area. I watched her training, dedication and loyalty to those in the military and the local community. I knew she had a thirst for knowledge and real-life experience, and that one day, she would be a leader. Jessica loved dogs and wanted to be a dog trainer when she grew up.

Mike, who I affectionately referred to as the "Dog Whisperer," was the owner and primary dog trainer of Halley's K9s for Veterans. Gavin was the Kennel Master and took care of all the dogs' needs. Pam was the compound manager and administrator. Together they taught Jessica about caring for and training the dogs, about social interaction with veterans, and about diversity of people with seen and unseen disabilities, during on-the-job volunteer training with homework requirements. Jessica gladly worked her hours and much more.

Previous to meeting Jessica, I attended a business networking meeting where I was mesmerized at how Mike Halley spoke to the group about his organization and the personal issues he and other veterans experienced. These issues included things such as: trouble sleeping; night terrors; family issues like divorce or issues with children and friends; and physical or health issues. He advanced many innovative thought processes, different techniques that he invisioned for all veterans participating in Halley's K9s for Veterans, especially veterans of the Afghanistan and Iraq wars.

Mike and I shared the same vision and thoughts regarding treatment of these veterans. I told him after the meeting that several Vietnam veterans had shared their worries with me in therapy, in order to possibly benefit some of the younger veterans I was seeing. They believed that the psychological toll of multiple deployments (many of which involved prolonged exposure to combat-related stress over multiple rotations), was terribly high compared with the physical injuries received in combat. I was extremely interested in Mike's program and wanted to volunteer my time and expertise to his organization.

I began to work with the staff, volunteers, and veterans at his compound, giving intensive individual therapy, group therapy, and marriage and family counseling, as well as Post-traumatic Stress Disorder (PTSD) and Traumatic Brain Injury (TBI) education, which comprised a large component of my therapeutic practice. Many clinical reports have referred to these as the signature wounds (PTSD & TBI) of the Afghanistan and Iraq conflicts, with the increasing concern about the incidence of suicide and suicide attempts among returning veterans.

As a humanitarian I am also concerned with military spouses and their need for more information on PTSD and TBI—as well as their need for family emotional health treatment before, during, and after deployments. Lastly, my heart goes out to the military children in need of treatment for coping with injured or deceased parent(s) as a result of war. Moreover, I share Jessica and her mother's (the author of this book) hope that this book can be inspirational to kids, and help them see that no matter how young, they can make a difference in the world—and that their voices and their actions are important.

Dr. Bev Jackson

My girl, Lola!

My name is Jessica and I'm 13 years old. This is the story of how I came to love (and leave) a dog named Lola.

I go to school at home with my twin brother, Josh, and we started eighth grade this year. Because we are homeschooled, we don't always sit at desks all day. We don't work out of textbooks much, and we don't spend a lot of time doing worksheets.

Doing School

We like to learn in lots of different ways. Sometimes we go on nature walks, visit foreign countries, go on field trips, or make crafts and cook things from books that we read.

I have always loved dogs and grew up with two miniature dachshunds named Sugar and Patches. But sadly they died in 2010 and 2011 when I was 11 and 12 years old.

After that we decided not to get more dogs of our own since my dad was in the military, and we moved every year to two years. Instead, when our friends and neighbors went on vacations, we took care of their dogs in our home.

I want to be a dog trainer some day when I grow up, so my Mom and I were talking about how I could get real experience training dogs as part of my homeschooling. We found out that you must be at least 16 to volunteer at most animal shelters and rescue places, and in some cases as old as 18. This was sad news for me, since I have a lot of years to go until I'm 18!

But then we found a place in town that rescues and trains big dogs as assistance dogs for military veterans who were hurt in wars. So, we went to check the place out to see if I could volunteer there a few days a week. We started by meeting the owners of the non-profit organization.

Mike, Owner; Pam, Manager; and Gavin, Kennel Master

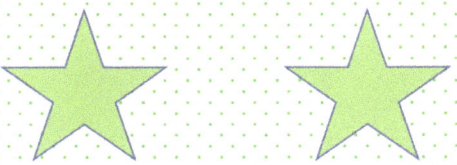

Kisses from Raine

They showed me the kennels where they keep the dogs that are eligible for training and asked me questions like, "Why do you want to train dogs?" I had no problem answering that question because I LOVE dogs and have an idea for a dog training business of my own when I grow up. Then I got to meet some of the dogs!

I was so happy when they invited me to become a regular volunteer. I started working there two days a week for two hours each time.

Mike, the owner and dog trainer, taught me a lot about how to walk a dog on the lead, and how to make it "stay," "sit," and "wait". I also learned a lot about how dogs are certified to be taken out in public by Assistance Dogs International.

Sometimes I'm required to scoop poop, help give baths, and clean dirty dog ears! I don't mind, though, because I know I'm helping the veterans, the dogs, and the organization. I also get to know the veterans who come to get assistance dogs and who stay for two weeks to learn how to train them.

Wash day

Meeting the veterans is one of the best parts of volunteering. Some have disabilities that can be seen, like limping, using a cane, or being in a wheelchair. Most, though, have disabilities that aren't as visible, like PTSD which stands for Post-Traumatic Stress Disorder.

People in the military have been fighting in many conflicts over the years, most recently in Afghanistan and Iraq. They sometimes see horrible sights and people getting badly hurt and are asked to do hard things that you or I could never do.

When they come back from war, sometimes they have a tough time sorting out all the bad things they have seen and all the hard things they were asked to do in order to defend our freedom. They can get confused about life, feel incredibly sad about buddies of theirs who died in combat, and can also get angry for reasons that we sometimes cannot understand.

When this happens, they often stop going out of their houses because they are afraid or get angry at inappropriate times. When they get an assistance dog, they get a faithful companion who loves them and serves them no matter what. The dog goes everywhere with them and helps to calm them down.

Tom and Bear

The dog also provides a bubble of space around the veteran that keeps people a little farther away, so the veteran feels safer and not so overwhelmed. Sometimes the dogs can do even more amazing things too, like wake the veteran up in the night when they begin to have a nightmare.

At the kennel I help walk the dogs and teach them basic commands, so they are ready for the veterans to take over when they come in to get their dogs. This is how I met the love of my life, Lola.

Lola is a tiger-striped Boxer who has a sweet nature and loves to give slobbery kisses. She has been at the kennel for quite a while and hasn't "chosen" a veteran yet or been chosen by one of them. The veterans seem to prefer the bigger Doberman Pinschers and German Shepherds as their service dogs, so Lola often does not get taken out to meet them.

I started walking Lola almost every time I volunteered, and she began to feel like my dog. She wiggles her whole behind with excitement when I go to her kennel to take her for a walk. When we take a break, she likes to sit with her paw on my foot and sometimes puts her head on my thigh to get scratched behind the ears.

I Love Lola!

After a few months went by, I found out there was another volunteer who liked to come and give Lola a romp. His name is Skip and he's in a wheelchair. He and Lola have been pals for quite a while.

One day, the owner of the organization decided to surprise Skip and offer Lola to him as his service dog. They brought Lola out to him with a special-made service dog vest and presented her to Skip. He was so excited and happy that he got down on the ground with her to wrestle and play.

Skip loves Lola!

When I saw their pictures on the Facebook site, I was so happy that Lola would finally have a fur-ever home and I knew that Skip loved her very much.

I knew when I started volunteering that I would sometimes have to say goodbye to dogs I loved. Though other dogs have come and gone, I didn't know I would love Lola so much, or that it would hurt so much to say goodbye.

She and Skip will have a happy life together and she will serve him faithfully. But I will miss her terribly. They have completed their training and tomorrow Skip will take Lola home forever, and I will go on volunteering and loving new dogs. Goodbye Lola girl. Thank you for being my friend.

AUTHOR'S NOTE FOR PARENTS AND TEACHERS:

Mike Halley was the owner of K9s for Veterans and a 100% disabled Vietnam Veteran. He had a special way of introducing the dogs (who were all rescue dogs) to a veteran and seeing which dog would "choose" the veteran. After that, the dog and the veteran went through a special bonding process and the veteran would spend the next two weeks learning to train their own dog. They would then return home to continue training to try to meet the criteria for certification. When they returned, they would be tested as a team. Because Mike and his partners were paying for the business out of their pockets and with somewhat meager donations, they were unable to continue the business after a few years and regrettably, had to shut it down, discontinuing their invaluable service to veterans.

Altogether I think they placed over 100 dogs with veterans (at no cost to the veterans except travel) who were then able to become more productive and functional members of society, some going to public places like restaurants and malls for the first time in decades. Sadly, Mike died in December of 2019, but his legacy of caring for and serving military veterans will live on. Semper Fi buddy. Rest in Peace.

ABOUT THE AUTHOR

 LIZ CIUFO is a former US Army paratrooper and US Army combat veteran of the Persian Gulf War (Desert Shield and Desert Storm) from August 1990—April of 1991, where she served with the XVIII Airborne Corps as an Intelligence Officer. She served six years of active duty in the US Army, four years in the US Army Reserve and thirteen years in the US Air Force Reserve, retiring as a Major in 2005. Elizabeth also holds a Master of Arts degree in Education and is a former middle school teacher.

During that time, Liz married a US Air Force officer and pilot and traipsed around the country with him and later, their two children (twins), for 24 years, homeschooling the twins, taking care of many airmen and their families, and being involved in many airmen and military family-oriented agencies and programs.

After retirement, Liz lived on a small hobby farm in northern California for a number of years, growing fruits, vegetables, and herbs, canning and preserving food, and raising sheep and chickens. She now lives with her young adult children in Las Vegas where she spends her time reading, writing, meeting with old friends who pass through town, and seeing the sights.

This book is Liz's first published work. It was followed by another children's book entitled, *Jessica's Dog, Cody*, and a non-fiction book which is a memoir of her time in Desert Storm called, *A Shoe in the Sand – A Look Behind for the Journey Ahead*. All are available on Amazon. Find Liz on the web at www.lizciufo.com and on Facebook at Liz Ciufo Author.

THINGS TO THINK ABOUT

1. What did you think the book was going to be about just looking at the title and the cover?

2. On Page 3, Dr. Bev says that no matter how young they are, kids can make a difference. What are some ways you could make a difference in the world? Look up some other stories online about kids who are doing interesting things and making a difference.

3. On page 6, Jessica talks about learning things in lots of different ways. Can you think of some other ways to learn something interesting other than from a teacher or from a textbook?

4. On page 12, Jessica begins to volunteer at the dog training place. Have you ever volunteered or wanted to volunteer? What are some things you could volunteer to do in your home, neighborhood, school, or town?

5. On pages 15 – 19 the book talks about military veterans and the ways they are sometimes hurt during a war, either physically or mentally. Do you know anyone who has served in the military—maybe one of your parents, grandparents, aunts or uncles, friends, or neighbors? If so, maybe you could try asking them what that experience was like for them.

6. On page 24, Skip is offered Lola as a service dog. Do you know anyone who has a service dog? Try looking up "Service Dogs for Veterans" on the internet and see what you can learn.

7. Do you think Jessica got over her broken heart from having to say goodbye to Lola?

8. On the page with the author's note for parents and teachers, the second to last sentence uses the words, "Semper Fi"

which is Latin, and short for "Semper Fidelis." Look up what that means and talk about why that is a good saying for a military person. Make up a motto for yourself.

9. On the last page about the author, were you surprised that she was a woman and a war veteran? Why or why not?

www.ingramcontent.com/pod-product-compliance
Lightning Source LLC
Chambersburg PA
CBHW042355070526
44585CB00028B/2940